Spelling and Vocabulary

1

Student Workbook

Author:

Mary Ellen Quint, Ph.D.

Editor:

Alan Christopherson, M.S.

Graphic Design:

Jennifer L. Davis, B.S.

Illustration:

Alpha Omega Creative Services

Alpha Omega Publications, Inc. • Rock Rapids, IA

Horizons Spelling and Vocabulary 1, Student Workbook
© MMI by Alpha Omega Publications, Inc.®
804 N. 2nd Ave. E.
Rock Rapids, IA 51246-1759

Printed in the United States of America

ISBN 978-0-7403-0212-1

Introduction

Welcome to the world of spelling words!

We use words almost every minute of every day, when we are awake, to tell people what we need, what we like, how we feel about things. When someone lives far away from us, or we don't see them very often, we often will write them a letter telling them about all the things that are happening in our lives. How can we write them a letter if we do not know how to put our words down on paper, if we do not know how to spell?

This year you will learn how to spell many of the words you use every day. You will learn some simple rules to help you with spelling words. You will learn that spelling is not just about putting one word down on paper by itself, but about everything that has to do with that word: what it means, how it fits with other words in sentences, and how you can use it in your writing.

You will learn to look for clues that will help you to spell new words that belong to the same "family" as the words you have already learned.

You will also learn about "working words." Working words include sight words, words selected by your class or your teacher for the week, and words that *you* want to learn.

Make sure your pencil is nice and sharp because this year you will learn how to better use words to communicate, as well as learning new words to use in your reading and writing.

Happy spelling!

Correct Right-Handed Position

Paper is placed on an angle to the left. Left hand steadies the paper and moves it up as you near the bottom of the page. Right hand is free to write.

Correct Left-Handed Position

Paper is placed on an angle to the right. Right hand steadies the paper and moves it up as you near the bottom of the page. Left hand is free to write. Watch hand positions carefully as shown in the picture.

Correct Hand and Pencil Position

Hold the pencil loosely about 1/2" to 1" above the sharpened point. Hold it between your thumb and index (pointer) finger. Let it rest on your middle finger. Do not grip the pencil tightly or your hand will become very tired. Do not let your hand slip down to the sharp point or you will have difficulty writing properly.

Correct Posture

Sit up tall, leaning slightly forward but not bending over your desk. Have your feet flat on the floor. Both arms will rest on the desk. Hold the paper with your free hand.

Correct Formation of Manuscript Letters and Numbers

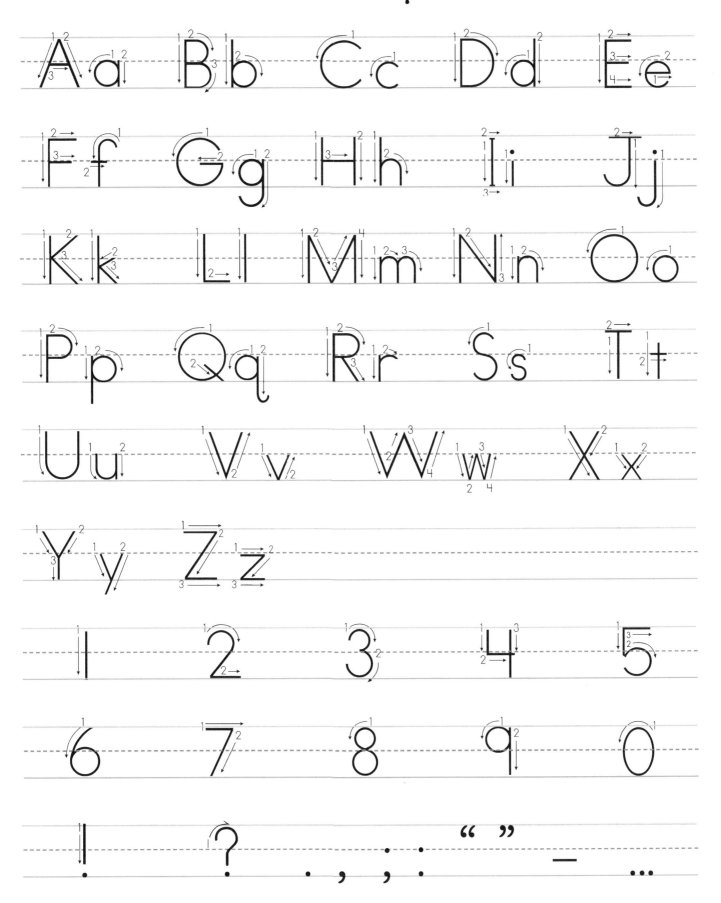

Good Spelling Begins Here...

1. *Read* the word and say it out loud.

2. *Think* about each sound in the word—close your eyes and say the word again.

3. *Spell* the word to yourself and then write it.

4. *Check* to see if you spelled the word correctly.

What do you know

Name: --

Write the words your teacher reads.

Words for the Week	Corrections	Practice
1.		1.
2.		2.
3.		3.
4.		4.
5.		5.
6.		6.
7.		7.
8.		8.
9.		9.
10.		10.
11.		11.
12.		12.

Words for the Week

an	and	bed	well	ten	I
am	cat	pen	yes	get	a

1 Write two sentences using your spelling words.

_____

- -

_____

- -

_____

2 Practice your spelling words. Don't forget your working words.

Horizons Spelling Grade 1

Lesson 1

Name: _____

Short ă and ĕ Words

✏ **Write the spelling words for the pictures.**

_____

_____

_____

_____

_____

_____

Spelling Words

an

am

and

cat

bed

pen

well

yes

ten

get

Working Words

I

a

Lesson 2

an	and	bed	well	ten	I
am	cat	pen	yes	get	a

 1 Write the words that begin with a short ă.

_____ _____ _____

_____ _____ _____

_____ _____ _____

 2 Write the words with only one letter.

_____ _____

_____ _____

_____ _____

 3 Write the short ĕ words.

_____ _____ _____

_____ _____ _____

_____ _____ _____

_____ _____ _____

4 Use your working words in a sentence.

_____

_____

_____

_____

Horizons Spelling Grade 1

Circle the word. Write it in the space.

1. am
   and

   I _____ happy.

2. get
   pen

   Do you write with a _____ ?

3. bed
   well

   Jesus met a woman getting water from a _____ .

4. ten
   yes

   Jesus healed _____ lepers.

5. an
   and

   You _____ I will go to the park.

Read Luke 17:11–19: Jesus cures ten lepers. Only one thanks Him.

Lesson 4   Name: _____

an	and	pen	ten	tan
am	cat	well	get	red
a	bed	yes	I	

Tell a friend about the cat in the picture. Use as many of your spelling words and your working words as you can.

_____

Dear _____ ,

_____

_____

_____

_____

_____

_____

Horizons Spelling Grade 1

Check-up time   Lesson 5

Name: --

Spelling Test	Corrections	Practice
1.		
2.		
3.		
4.		
5.		
6.		
7.		
8.		
9.		
10.		
11.		
12.		

Test Again

More Practice

What do you know?

Name: ------------------------------

Write the words your teacher reads.

Words for the Week	Corrections	Practice
1.		1.
2.		2.
3.		3.
4.		4.
5.		5.
6.		6.
7.		7.
8.		8.
9.		9.
10.		10.
11.		11.
12.		12.

Words for the Week

will	his	in	on	God	have
did	it	hop	not	mom	come

1 Write two sentences using your spelling words.

_____

- -

_____

_____

- -

2 Practice your spelling words. Don't forget your working words.

14

Lesson 6

Short Ĭ and Ŏ Words

Name: _____

1 What shape is the word?

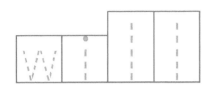
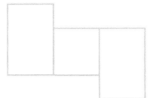

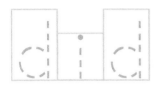

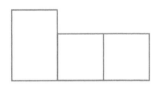

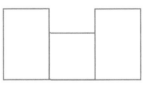

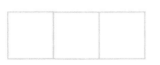

2 Draw the shapes of your working words.

Spelling Words

will

did

his

it

in

hop

on

not

God

mom

Working Words

have

come

Lesson 7

Name: _____

1. Circle the short ŏ words.

will	his	in	on	God	have
did	it	hop	not	mom	come

2. Write the spelling word that rhymes.

lid _____

rod _____

bit _____

is _____

hot _____

Tom _____

hill _____

mop _____

Don _____

win _____

3. Write the working words.

_____   _____

_____   _____

Lesson 8

Name: _____

1 Use the words in sentences.

| will | it | did | in | his | have |

1. John lost _____ ball.

2. I _____ a new coat.

3. We _____ go to church.

4. Jill was _____ the car.

5. I saw a rainbow. Did you see _____ ?

6. Yes, I _____ .

2 Write the Bible verse: God is love. Whoever lives in love lives in God, and God in him.
1 John 4:16

_____

_____

_____

_____

Lesson 9

Name: _____

will	on
did	not
his	God
it	mom
in	have
hop	come

✏ **Write a letter to God about your mom.**

Dear God,

_____

_____

_____

_____

_____

_____

_____

Love,

_____

Horizons Spelling Grade 1

Check-up time

Lesson 10

Name: _____

Spelling Test	Corrections	Practice
1.		
2.		
3.		
4.		
5.		
6.		
7.		
8.		
9.		
10.		
11.		
12.		

Test Again

More Practice

Name:

Write the words your teacher reads.

Words for the Week	Corrections	Practice
1.		1.
2.		2.
3.		3.
4.		4.
5.		5.
6.		6.
7.		7.
8.		8.
9.		9.
10.		10.
11.		11.
12.		12.

Words for the Week

run	but	just	city	gentle	the
up	sun	us	cent	can	they

1 Write two sentences using your spelling words.

_____

- -

_____

- -

_____

2 Practice your spelling words. Don't forget your working words.

Horizons Spelling Grade 1

Lesson 11   Name:

Short ŭ, soft c, g Words

✎ **Trace and match.**

1. run

2. sun

3. city

4. cent

5. us

6. up

Spelling Words

run

up

but

sun

just

us

city

cent

gentle

can

Working Words

the

they

 **Spelling Spotlight**

Lesson 12   Name: _____

run	but	just	city	gentle	the
up	sun	us	cent	can	they

1 Find two spelling words that rhyme. Write them.

_____   _____

2 Find two soft c words. Write them.

_____   _____

3 Find two words that begin with *th*. Write them.

_____   _____

4 Find one soft g word. Write it.   **5** Find one hard c word. Write it.

_____   _____

 6 Circle the short ŭ words.

up	they	sun
can	just	gentle
but	city	us

Lesson 13

 Use a spelling word to replace the word on the lines.

run	but	just	city	gentle
up	sun	us	cent	can

1. I will _____ walk _____ home.

2. The _____ moon _____ is very hot.

3. We live in the _____ hills _____.

4. Jill had only one _____ penny _____.

5. We walked _____ down _____ the hill.

6. The puppy was _____ lively _____.

 Bible Verse: (God) made the great lights...the sun to govern the day...the moon and stars to govern the night.

Psalm 136:7–9

Lesson 14   Name: _____

run
up
but
sun
just
us
city
cent
gentle
can

Write a short story about the picture. Use words from the lesson and your own words.

The City

Horizons Spelling Grade 1

Check-up time   Lesson 15   Name:

Spelling Test	Corrections	Practice
1.		
2.		
3.		
4.		
5.		
6.		
7.		
8.		
9.		
10.		
11.		
12.		

Lesson 15

Name: _____

Test Again	More Practice

Name: _____

Write the words your teacher reads.

Words for the Week	Corrections	Practice
1.		1.
2.		2.
3.		3.
4.		4.
5.		5.
6.		6.
7.		7.
8.		8.
9.		9.
10.		10.
11.		11.
12.		12.

Words for the Week

came	made	play	rain	say	said
make	day	sail	mail	gate	are

1 Write two sentences using your spelling words.

_____

- -

_____

- -

_____

2 Practice your spelling words. Don't forget your working words.

Horizons Spelling Grade 1

Spelling Spotlight

Lesson 16
Long ā Words

Name: _____

came

make

made

day

play

sail

rain

mail

say

gate

Working Words

said

are

1 Three ways to spell long ā. Write the words.

_____ a _____ e

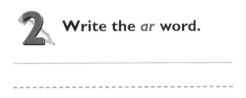

_____ ai _____

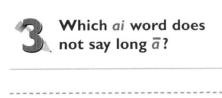

_____ ay

2 Write the *ar* word.

3 Which *ai* word does not say long ā?

Spelling Spotlight

Lesson 17   Name: ----------------------

1. Write the word for the picture.

came	made	play	rain	say	said
make	day	sail	mail	gate	are

2. Write the spelling word that rhymes with the picture.

1. Write the spelling word that is opposite.

night

sun

work

went

2. Finish the sentences. Use the words in the box.

made	said	are	say	make

1. Joe _____ , "How _____ you?"

2. I _____ that drawing.

3. Did you _____ a hat for the party?

4. What did you _____ to me?

Bible Verse: Jesus said, "I am the gate for the sheep...I am the gate; whoever enters through me will be saved."
John 10:7, 9

Lesson 19

Name: _____

came
make
made
day
play
sail
rain
mail
say
gate
said
are

Write a story about the picture.

A Day in the Rain

 **Lesson 20**   Name:

Spelling Test	Corrections	Practice
1.		
2.		
3.		
4.		
5.		
6.		
7.		
8.		
9.		
10.		
11.		
12.		

Lesson 20

Name:

Test Again	More Practice

Write the words your teacher reads.

Words for the Week	Corrections	Practice
1.		1.
2.		2.
3.		3.
4.		4.
5.		5.
6.		6.
7.		7.
8.		8.
9.		9.
10.		10.
11.		11.
12.		12.

Words for the Week

be	he	eat	meal	feet	mother
see	me	read	tree	three	father

1 Write two sentences using your spelling words.

_____

_____

_____

_____

2 Practice your spelling words. Don't forget your working words.

_____

_____

_____

_____

_____

_____

_____

_____

_____

_____

_____

_____

Lesson 21
Long ē Words

Name: _____

1 Write the long ē words spelled with **ee**.

_____   _____

_____   _____

_____   _____

2 Write the long ē words spelled with **ea**.

_____

_____

_____

_____

_____

3 Write the long ē words spelled with **e**.

_____   _____

_____   _____

4 Write the working words for parents.

_____

_____

_____

5 Write your other working words.

_____   _____

_____   _____

Spelling Words

be

see

he

me

eat

read

meal

tree

feet

three

Working Words

mother

father

Lesson 22   Name: _____

✏️ **Write the word for the picture.**

be	he	eat	meal	feet	mother
see	me	read	tree	three	father

_____

_____

_____

Bible Verse: Honor your father and mother, so that you may live long in the land the LORD your God is giving you.

Exodus 20:12

Lesson 23   Name: _____

1 **Use the six rhyming words in sentences.**

three	be	see	he	me	tree

1. Will _____ go with us to the store?

2. Jim will _____ here at _____ o'clock.

3. Did you _____ Bob climb the _____?

4. Watch _____ run.

2 **Circle the word. Write it in the sentence.**

1. meal
   meet

   We had ham for our evening _____.

2. real
   read

   How many books did you _____?

3. mother
   matter

   Mary's _____ baked cookies.

4. ear
   eat

   We will _____ supper at six.

5. feather
   father

   Jim's _____ will coach the team.

Lesson 24 Name: _____

be
see
he
me
eat
read
meal
tree
feet
three
mother
father

 Write a story about the picture.

The Evening Meal

Check-up time Lesson 25 Name: _____

Spelling Test	Corrections	Practice
1.		
2.		
3.		
4.		
5.		
6.		
7.		
8.		
9.		
10.		
11.		
12.		

Test Again

More Practice

What do you know

Name: _____

Write the words your teacher reads.

Words for the Week	Corrections	Practice
1.		1.
2.		2.
3.		3.
4.		4.
5.		5.
6.		6.
7.		7.
8.		8.
9.		9.
10.		10.
11.		11.
12.		12.

Words for the Week

like	time	tie	mile	my	was
hide	pie	eye	find	mine	were

1 Write two sentences using your spelling words.

_____

- -

_____

- -

_____

2 Practice your spelling words. Don't forget your working words.

Spelling Spotlight

Lesson 26
Long T Words

Name: _____

Spelling Words

like
hide
time
pie
tie
eye
mile
find
my
mine

Working Words

was
were

1 Write the two words with the same shape.

1.

2.

2 Match the word to its shape and write it.

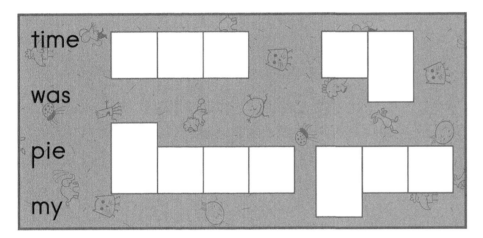

time

was

pie

my

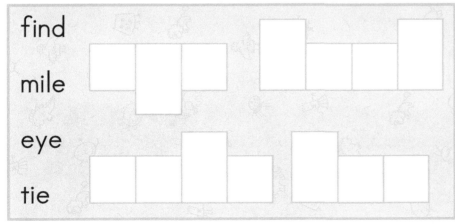

find

mile

eye

tie

3 Draw the shapes for your working words.

Lesson 27   Name: _____

1 Circle the hidden word and write it on the line.

like	time	tie	mile	my	was
hide	pie	eye	find	mine	were

1. xvtierz _____

2. mneyel _____

3. yuimyw _____

4. ppieer _____

5. aslikerz _____

2 Change the words below to spelling words.

hid _____   Tim _____

3 Write the two *w* words.

_____   _____

4 Write the four words that rhyme.

_____   _____

_____   _____

48

Horizons Spelling Grade 1

Spelling Spotlight

1 **Look at the picture. Finish the sentence.**

John can walk a _____ .
               mile   mine

If I _____ , will you _____ me?
    find   hide   find   hide

What _____ is it?
     like   time

Al and Ann _____ going to church.
       was   were

This is _____ puppy.
    my   mine

2 **Use your working words in a sentence.**

_____

_____

_____

_____

**Bible Verse: O Lord, Keep me as the apple of your eye; hide me in the
shadow of your wings.**

Psalm 17:8

Lesson 29   Name: _____

like
hide
time
pie
tie
eye
mile
find
my
mine
was
were

✏ **Write a story about the picture.**

Hide and Seek

Lesson 30   Name: _____

Spelling Test	Corrections	Practice
1.		
2.		
3.		
4.		
5.		
6.		
7.		
8.		
9.		
10.		
11.		
12.		

Test Again	More Practice

What do you know

Lessons 31–35

Name:

Write the words your teacher reads.

Words for the Week	Corrections	Practice
1.		1.
2.		2.
3.		3.
4.		4.
5.		5.
6.		6.
7.		7.
8.		8.
9.		9.
10.		10.
11.		11.
12.		12.

Words for the Week

go   stone   old   boat   zero   do

so   home   toe   goat   hope   Jesus

1 Write two sentences using your spelling words.

2 Practice your spelling words. Don't forget your working words.

Lesson 31
Long ō Words

Name: _____

1 Write the missing vowels.

st__n__   b__ __ __t

z__r__   h__ __m__

g__ __t   t__ __ __

2 Write your working words. Circle the vowels.

Spelling Words

go

so

stone

home

old

toe

boat

goat

zero

hope

Working Words

do

Jesus

Lesson 32   Name:

1 Find the picture for the word. Color the picture. Draw a line to the word.

goat   home   zero   stone   boat   toe

2 Find the long $\bar{o}$ pattern. Write the words.

___ o ___ e	___ o	___ oa ___

Write the spelling word in the sentence.

goat	toe	Jesus	zero	home	old
hope	boat	go	so	do	stone

1. We went sailing in a _____ .

2. How _____ are you?

3. What will you _____ today?

4. I hurt my _____ .

5. _____ died for us.

6. The _____ ate my lunch.

7. We _____ that we can

go to the party.

Lesson 34   Name: _____

Bible Story: *Jesus Calms the Sea* **– Luke 8:22–25. Draw a picture and tell a friend about Jesus and the storm at sea.**

Dear _____ ,

Love,

Lesson 35

Name: _____

Spelling Test	Corrections	Practice
1.		
2.		
3.		
4.		
5.		
6.		
7.		
8.		
9.		
10.		
11.		
12.		

Check-up time Lesson 35 Name:

Test Again	More Practice

Write the words your teacher reads.

1. _____

2. _____

3. _____

4. _____

5. _____

6. _____

7. _____

8. _____

9. _____

10. _____

11. _____

12. _____

13. _____

14. _____

15. _____

16. _____

17. _____

18. _____

19. _____

20. _____

21. _____

22. _____

23. _____

24. _____

25. _____

26. _____

27. _____

28. _____

Review Words

and	God	the	said	read	were	Jesus
well	did	but	yes	three	like	home
get	have	can	are	mother	was	do
will	they	came	made	father	mine	boat

Practice all the words you have learned so far.

Spelling Spotlight

Lesson 36
Review

Name: _____

and	God	the	said	read	were	Jesus
well	did	but	yes	three	like	home
get	have	can	are	mother	was	do
will	they	came	made	father	mine	boat

1. Write the words with the short ă sound.

_____

4. Write the words with the long ē sound.

_____

2. Write the words with the long ā sound.

_____

6. Write the words with the long ī sound.

_____

7. Write the words with the short ŏ sound.

_____

3. Write the words with the short ĕ sound.

_____

5. Write the words with the short ĭ sound.

_____

8. Write the words with the long ō sound.

_____

 **Spelling Spotlight**

Lesson 37   Name: _____

and	God	the	said	read	were	Jesus
well	did	but	yes	three	like	home
get	have	can	are	mother	was	do
will	they	came	made	father	mine	boat

1 Write the words in the sentences.

Mother said, "Jill, where _____ you when it

_____ _____ _____

_____ time to _____ _____ chores?"

_____ _____ _____

Jill _____ , "I _____ home, _____

_____

I forgot to _____ them."

2 Find a review word that rhymes. (Listen to the sound. Spellings will be different.)

bell _____   tree _____

goat _____   hay _____

seed _____   hid _____

bike _____   nut _____

bed _____   fine _____

foam _____   car _____

1. Use the words in a sentence.

| Jesus | father |

_____

_____

| made | mother |

_____

_____

| well | get | and |

_____

_____

| three | read |

_____

_____

2. Put the words in **ABC** order.

| but | and | came | mine | do | the |

1. _____   4. _____

2. _____   5. _____

3. _____   6. _____

Lesson 39

Name: _____

and	God	the	said	read	were	Jesus
well	did	but	yes	three	like	home
get	have	can	are	mother	was	do
will	they	came	made	father	mine	boat

Write a story using as many spelling words as you can. Circle the words in the box when you use them.

Horizons Spelling Grade 1

Write the words your teacher reads.

1. _____

2. _____

3. _____

4. _____

5. _____

6. _____

7. _____

8. _____

9. _____

10. _____

11. _____

12. _____

13. _____

14. _____

15. _____

16. _____

17. _____

18. _____

19. _____

20. _____

21. _____

22. _____

23. _____

24. _____

25. _____

26. _____

27. _____

28. _____

Lesson 40

Name: --------------------------------

Test Again

More Practice

Horizons Spelling Grade 1

What do you know?

Name: --

Write the words your teacher reads.

Words for the Week	Corrections	Practice
1.		1.
2.		2.
3.		3.
4.		4.
5.		5.
6.		6.
7.		7.
8.		8.
9.		9.
10.		10.
11.		11.
12.		12.

Words for the Week

you	cute	blue	fix	X-ray	love
tube	use	box	ax	fox	your

1 Write two sentences using your spelling words.

_____

_____

_____

_____

2 Practice your spelling words. Don't forget your working words.

Spelling Spotlight

Lesson 41 Name:
Long ū Words; x Sounds

1 Write and match.

1. box

2. tube

3. ax

4. X-ray

5. fox

6. blue

2 Write your working words.

Spelling Words

you
tube
cute
use
blue
box
fox
ax
X-ray
fix

Working Words
love
your

Spelling Spotlight

Lesson 42   Name: _____

1 **Write the long ū words in the shapes.**

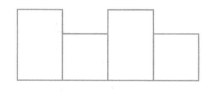      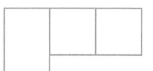

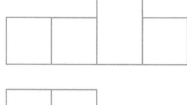

2 **Write the word that rhymes.**

| you | cute | blue | fix | X-ray | love |
| tube | use | box | ax | fox | your |

mix   _____

play   _____

flute _____

lox   _____

tax   _____

four   _____

cube   _____

shoe   _____

Circle the word. Write it in the sentence.

1. live
   love

God is _____ .

2. you
   your

Is this _____ bike?

3. cute
   tube

The baby is _____ .

4. blue
   box

The sky is _____ .

5. use
   ax

I can _____ a pen.

6. ax
   ask

Can you find the _____ ?

Bible Verse: A new command I give you: Love one another. As I have loved you, so you must love one another.   **John 13:34**

Write the verse.

_____

_____

_____

_____

_____

Lesson 44 Name:

1 Write about it.

I love

2 Draw a picture.

Horizons Spelling Grade 1

Check-up time Lesson 45   Name:

Spelling Test	Corrections	Practice
1.		
2.		
3.		
4.		
5.		
6.		
7.		
8.		
9.		
10.		
11.		
12.		

Lesson 45

Name:

Test Again

More Practice

Write the words your teacher reads.

Words for the Week	Corrections	Practice
1.		1.
2.		2.
3.		3.
4.		4.
5.		5.
6.		6.
7.		7.
8.		8.
9.		9.
10.		10.
11.		11.
12.		12.

Words for the Week

I'm you're we'll don't miss friend

I've I'll can't add tall too

1 Write two sentences using your spelling words.

2 Practice your spelling words. Don't forget your working words.

Horizons Spelling Grade 1

Lesson 46
Contractions, Double Consonants

Name: _____

1 Write the contraction.

1. I am _____

2. do not _____

3. we will _____

4. I have _____

5. cannot _____

6. I will _____

7. you are _____

2 Write your working words.

_____ _____

_____

_____

Spelling Words

I'm
I've
you're
I'll
we'll
can't
don't
add
miss
tall

Working Words

friend
too

Spelling Spotlight

Lesson 47   Name: _____

1 Write the word.

I'm	you're	we'll	don't	miss	friend
I've	I'll	can't	add	tall	too

1. I _____ my lost pet.

2. Jesus is your _____ .

3. The pine tree grew very _____ .

4. 1 + 1 = 2 _____

5. Jill will go to the play with us, _____ .

2 Which contraction is it?

Two contractions with *not*.   _____   _____

Two contractions with *will*.   _____   _____

One contraction with *have*.   _____

One contraction with *are*.   _____

Horizons Spelling Grade 1

Spelling Spotlight

Lesson 48   Name: _____

✎ **Write the mixed-up sentence in the right order. Don't forget the period!**

ball   I've   a   red   got

_____

miss   friend   my   I

_____

table   too   The   tall   is

_____

going   I'm   school   to

_____

add   He   can't   this

_____

Bible Verse: Jesus answered, "I am the way and the truth and the life."
John 14:6

Draw a picture of your friend. Then write a story about your friend.

My Friend

Check-up time

Lesson 50

Name: _____

Spelling Test	Corrections	Practice
1.		
2.		
3.		
4.		
5.		
6.		
7.		
8.		
9.		
10.		
11.		
12.		

Test Again

More Practice

Write the words your teacher reads.

Words for the Week	Corrections	Practice
1.		1.
2.		2.
3.		3.
4.		4.
5.		5.
6.		6.
7.		7.
8.		8.
9.		9.
10.		10.
11.		11.
12.		12.

Words for the Week

walls	eggs	dresses	classes	beaches	very
dolls	boxes	wishes	lunches	dishes	people

1 Write two sentences using your spelling words.

_____

- -

_____

- -

_____

2 Practice your spelling words. Don't forget your working words.

Horizons Spelling Grade 1

Lesson 51
Plurals (-s, -es)

Name: _____

Spelling Words

walls

dolls

eggs

boxes

dresses

wishes

classes

lunches

beaches

dishes

Working Words

very

people

1 **Write the plural.**

dress _____

lunch _____

dish _____

egg _____

doll _____

person _____

box _____

class _____

beach _____

wish _____

wall _____

Lesson 52   Name: _____

| walls | eggs | dresses | classes | beaches | very |
| dolls | boxes | wishes | lunches | dishes | people |

1 **Find a spelling word that rhymes.**

balls _____

glasses _____

legs _____

bunches _____

foxes _____

peaches _____

fishes _____

Mary _____

2 **Write the words.**

| dolls | dresses | very | people |

Some _____ like to collect _____ .

Jack likes pizza _____ much.

All the girls had new _____
for the party.

Lesson 53   Name: _____

1 Find the words. Circle, write, and match.

faboxess   _____

lyeggsz   _____

bbdressessz   _____

dxdishesyz   _____

atclassesmb   _____

2 Finish the sentence. Circle the word and write it.

Mother packed _____ for school.

    dishes   lunches

Sue was _____ happy.

    very   wary

Molly has many _____ .

    walls   dolls

The _____ painted the _____ .

    pets   people   wishes   walls

Lesson 54   Name: _____

✏️ **Write a story that tells what Jesus did with five loaves and two fishes.**

Jesus Feeds the People

Horizons Spelling Grade 1

Lesson 55

Name:

Spelling Test	Corrections	Practice
1.		
2.		
3.		
4.		
5.		
6.		
7.		
8.		
9.		
10.		
11.		
12.		

Test Again	More Practice

What do you know

Lessons 56–60

Name:

Write the words your teacher reads.

Words for the Week	Corrections	Practice
1.		1.
2.		2.
3.		3.
4.		4.
5.		5.
6.		6.
7.		7.
8.		8.
9.		9.
10.		10.
11.		11.
12.		12.

Words for the Week

longer   fastest   higher   longest   softest   some

faster   kinder   highest   softer   kindest   most

1   **Write two sentences using your spelling words.**

2   **Practice your spelling words. Don't forget your working words.**

Horizons Spelling Grade 1

1 Write the spelling words that go with each word.

long   soft

_____   _____

_____   _____

kind   high

_____   _____

_____   _____

fast

_____

_____

2 Write your working words.

_____   _____

_____   _____

Spelling Words

longer

faster

fastest

kinder

higher

highest

longest

softer

softest

kindest

Working Words

some

most

Lesson 57   Name:

1. Circle the spelling words.

s	l	a	x	t	l	a	b	k
b	o	x	h	m	o	s	t	i
l	n	f	a	s	t	e	r	n
o	g	a	t	d	e	f	h	d
n	e	s	g	e	h	k	i	e
g	r	t	l	j	r	l	g	s
e	k	e	t	l	m	l	h	t
s	p	s	k	i	n	d	e	r
t	r	t	r	s	t	o	r	u
s	o	m	e	v	w	x	y	z

longer

faster

kinder

higher

longest

softer

fastest

kindest

some

most

2. Use your working words in a sentence.

_____

_____

_____

_____

Circle the word.

1. The car is (**fastest faster**) than the dog.

2. The blue car is the (**faster fastest**).

3. (**Some Most**) of the blocks are blue.

4. (**Some Most**) of the blocks are red.

5. The green kite is the (**higher highest**).

6. The red ribbon is (**longer longest**) than the blue ribbon.

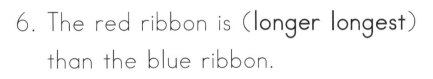
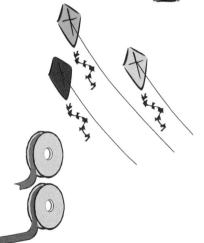

Bible Verse: Glory to God in the highest, and on earth peace to men on whom his favor rests.

Luke 2:14

Lesson 59   Name: _____

1 Write about it and draw a picture.

The softest

2 Write about it and draw a picture.

The kindest person I know
is

Horizons Spelling Grade 1

Spelling Test	Corrections	Practice
1.		
2.		
3.		
4.		
5.		
6.		
7.		
8.		
9.		
10.		
11.		
12.		

Check-up time   Lesson 60   Name:

Test Again	More Practice

What do you know

Name: _____

Write the words your teacher reads.

Words for the Week	Corrections	Practice
1.		1.
2.		2.
3.		3.
4.		4.
5.		5.
6.		6.
7.		7.
8.		8.
9.		9.
10.		10.
11.		11.
12.		12.

Words for the Week

cupful	playful	looking	trying	kindness	Christmas
handful	calling	spelling	goodness	happiness	other

1 Write two sentences using your spelling words.

_____

- -

_____

- -

_____

2 Practice your spelling words. Don't forget your working words.

Horizons Spelling Grade 1

Lesson 61

Name: _____

Suffixes: -ful, -ing, -ness

1 Trace the word and match.

1. cup

2. handful

3. spelling

4. Christmas

5. cupful

6. hand

c-a-t

Spelling Words

cupful

handful

playful

calling

looking

spelling

trying

goodness

kindness

happiness

Working Words

Christmas

other

2 Write your working words.

Lesson 62

Name: _____

✏ **Write the words.**

 cup + ful _____

 play + ful _____

 hand + ful _____

 call + ing _____

 look + ing _____

d–o–g spell + ing _____

 try + ing _____

 kind + ness _____

 good + ness _____

 happy – y + i + ness _____

other	Christmas	goodness
calling	kindness	happiness

1 **Write the words.**

1. Psalm 23 tells us that only _____ and

_____ will follow us all the days of our life.

2. Jesus' birthday is _____ day.

3. Mother is _____ John in for supper.

4. The _____ children will come tonight.

2 **Use your working words in a sentence.**

1. _____

_____

2. _____

Bible Verse: Today in the town of David a Savior has been born to you; he is Christ the Lord. This will be a sign to you: you will find a baby wrapped in cloths and lying in a manger.   **Luke 2:11-12**

Lesson 64

Name: ---------------------------------

✏️ Christmas is a time of *happiness, kindness,* and *goodness.* Draw a picture and write a Christmas story using these words.

cupful
handful
playful
calling
looking
spelling
trying
goodness
kindness
happiness
Christmas
other

Horizons Spelling Grade 1

Lesson 65   Name:

Spelling Test	Corrections	Practice
1.		
2.		
3.		
4.		
5.		
6.		
7.		
8.		
9.		
10.		
11.		
12.		

Check-up time

Lesson 65

Name: _____

Test Again	More Practice

Write the words your teacher reads.

Words for the Week	Corrections	Practice
1.		1.
2.		2.
3.		3.
4.		4.
5.		5.
6.		6.
7.		7.
8.		8.
9.		9.
10.		10.
11.		11.
12.		12.
13.		13.
14.		14.

Words for the Week

| back | high | knock | whole | sign | lamb | Mr. |
| night | light | know | write | gnat | climb | Mrs. |

1 Write two sentences using your spelling words.

_____

- -

_____

- -

_____

- -

2 Practice your spelling words. Don't forget your working words.

Horizons Spelling Grade 1

Lesson 66

Silent Letters

Name: _____

 Write the words.

-igh	kn-

-mb	gn- -gn

-ck	wr- wh-

2 **Write your working words.**

Spelling Words

back
night
high
light
knock
know
whole
write
sign
gnat
lamb
climb

Working Words

Mr.
Mrs.

Lesson 67

Name: _____

1 Put the words in **ABC** order.

light
gnat
back
knock
night
climb

1. _____

2. _____

3. _____

4. _____

5. _____

6. _____

2 Write the abbreviations. Don't forget the period!

Mister = _____

Mistress = _____

3 Cross out the silent letter or letters in each word.

back	knock	sign	night
know	gnat	high	whole
lamb	light	write	climb

Horizons Spelling Grade 1

1 Use the words in a sentence.

lamb   climb

know   write

sign   high

2 Write your working words in a sentence.

Bible Verse: John (the Baptist) saw Jesus coming toward him and said, "Look, the Lamb of God, who takes away the sin of the world!"

John 1:29

Lesson 69

Name: _____

✏ **Write a story about:** *The night the gnat knocked over the light.*

back

night

high

light

knock

know

whole

write

sign

gnat

lamb

climb

Mr.

Mrs.

Horizons Spelling Grade 1

Check-up time Lesson 70 Name:

Spelling Test	Corrections	Practice
1.		1.
2.		2.
3.		3.
4.		4.
5.		5.
6.		6.
7.		7.
8.		8.
9.		9.
10.		10.
11.		11.
12.		12.
13.		13.
14.		14.

Check-up time

Lesson 70

Name: _____

Test Again	More Practice

Lessons 71–75

Name: ----------------------------------

Write the words your teacher reads.

Words for the Week	Corrections	Practice
1.		1.
2.		2.
3.		3.
4.		4.
5.		5.
6.		6.
7.		7.
8.		8.
9.		9.
10.		10.
11.		11.
12.		12.
13.		13.
14.		14.

Words for the Week

book	foot	tooth	zoo	peace	bread	brother
good	food	moon	sea	head	great	sister

1 Write two sentences using your spelling words.

_____

_____

_____

_____

2 Practice your spelling words. Don't forget your working words.

1 What do you hear?

oo =   oo =

b ____ ____ k   m ____ ____ n

g ____ ____ d   f ____ ____ d

f ____ ____ t   z ____ ____

   t ____ ____ th

ea = ē   ea = ĕ

s ____ ____   h ____ ____ d

p ____ ____ ce   br ____ ____ d

ea = ā

gr ____ ____ t

2 Write your working words.

_____   _____

_____   _____

_____   _____

Spelling Words

book
good
foot
food
tooth
moon
zoo
sea
peace
head
bread
great

Working Words

brother
sister

Spelling Spotlight

Lesson 72   Name: _____

Write the spelling word for the picture.

book	foot	tooth	zoo	peace	bread	brother
good	food	moon	sea	head	great	sister

_____

_____

_____

_____

_____

_____

_____

_____

_____

Horizons Spelling Grade 1

1 **Write the spelling word that is the opposite.**

bad

war

less

brother

sister

2 **Write the spelling words in the puzzle.**

zoo

food

book

bread

sister

foot

brother

head

great

sea

peace

tooth

good

ACROSS:
1. Something you read.
3. James was John's _____ .
6. Opposite of bad.
8. Jesus said, "_____ be with you."
10. Martha was Mary's _____ .
13. What we eat.

DOWN:
2. I hop on one _____ .
4. We use _____ to make a sandwich.
5. Rhymes with 8.
7. I lost my first _____ .
9. A large body of water.
11. Animals live here.
12. Use your _____ !

Lesson 74   Name: _____

Jesus gives us peace. Read John 14:27; 20:19, 21, and 26.

Draw a picture of your family. Write a letter to Jesus asking Him to give peace to your family.

Dear Jesus,

Check-up time   Lesson 75   Name: _____

Spelling Test	Corrections	Practice
1.		1.
2.		2.
3.		3.
4.		4.
5.		5.
6.		6.
7.		7.
8.		8.
9.		9.
10.		10.
11.		11.
12.		12.
13.		13.
14.		14.

Check-up time

Lesson 75

Name: _____

Test Again	More Practice

Name: ------------------

Write the words your teacher reads.

1. _____

2. _____

3. _____

4. _____

5. _____

6. _____

7. _____

8. _____

9. _____

10. _____

11. _____

12. _____

13. _____

14. _____

15. _____

16. _____

17. _____

18. _____

19. _____

20. _____

21. _____

22. _____

23. _____

24. _____

25. _____

26. _____

27. _____

28. _____

Review Words

your	friend	very	some	other	night	good
love	can't	people	most	playful	write	great
blue	I'm	classes	kindest	happiness	back	sister
you	you're	boxes	faster	spelling	know	brother

Practice your review words.

Horizons Spelling Grade 1

your	friend	very	some	other	night	good
love	can't	people	most	playful	write	great
blue	I'm	classes	kindest	happiness	back	sister
you	you're	boxes	faster	spelling	know	brother

1 Find 3 contractions. Write them. Write what they stand for.

------------- = -------------

------------- = -------------

------------- = -------------

2 Circle the silent letter or letters in the words.

love   back   write   some

friend   blue   great   know

night   people   you

3 Put the words in ABC order.

good	great	blue	people	classes	night

1. -------------   4. -------------

2. -------------   5. -------------

3. -------------   6. -------------

Spelling Spotlight

Lesson 77   Name: _____

your	friend	very	some	other	night	good
love	can't	people	most	playful	write	great
blue	I'm	classes	kindest	happiness	back	sister
you	you're	boxes	faster	spelling	know	brother

1 **Write the word that rhymes.**

rack _____   mother _____

Mary _____   Mister _____

light _____   go _____

foxes _____   ate _____

host _____   come _____

2 **Write the word.**

1. most kind _____

2. nice and kind _____

3. a color _____

4. cannot _____

5. more than 1 box _____

6. opposite of front _____

Horizons Spelling Grade 1

 Write a sentence using the words.

happiness

playful   you

spelling

friend   love

classes

people   faster

back   I'm

Lesson 79   Name:

love   happiness   brother   know   most   people
friend   sister   good   great   kindest   some

Write a story. Use the spelling words in the box.

Lesson 80

Name: _____

Write the words your teacher reads.

1. _____

2. _____

3. _____

4. _____

5. _____

6. _____

7. _____

8. _____

9. _____

10. _____

11. _____

12. _____

13. _____

14. _____

15. _____

16. _____

17. _____

18. _____

19. _____

20. _____

21. _____

22. _____

23. _____

24. _____

25. _____

26. _____

27. _____

28. _____

Test Again

More Practice

What do you know

Name: --

Write the words your teacher reads.

Words for the Week	Corrections	Practice
1.		1.
2.		2.
3.		3.
4.		4.
5.		5.
6.		6.
7.		7.
8.		8.
9.		9.
10.		10.
11.		11.
12.		12.
13.		13.
14.		14.

Words for the Week

out	about	down	yellow	Paul	yawn	one
our	house	now	bowl	saw	straw	from

1 Write two sentences using your spelling words.

---

2 Practice your spelling words. Don't forget your working words.

Horizons Spelling Grade 1

Spelling Spotlight

Lesson 81   Name: _____

ou, ow, au, aw Words

1 Match the shape to the word. Match the word to the picture.

   yellow

   house

   bowl

   down

   yawn

   straw

2 Write the working word and draw the shape.

_____

_____

_____

_____

Spelling Words

out
our
about
house
down
now
yellow
bowl
Paul
saw
yawn
straw

Working Words

one
from

Lesson 82   Name:

Unscramble the words and write them.

aws

osehu

lPua

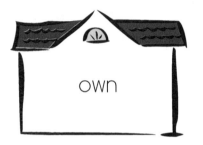
own

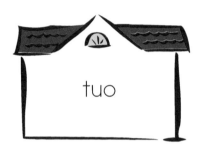
tuo

btaou

ruo

eno

rmof

wlloey

wyan

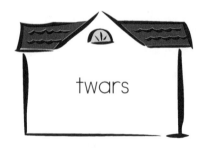
twars

Horizons Spelling Grade 1

Spelling Spotlight

Lesson 83   Name:

Unscramble the sentence and write it. Don't forget the period!

house   yellow   My   is

yawn   saw   I   Paul

the   now   down   Put   straw   of   bowl

boy   One   came   door   of   the   out

lives   She   our   near   house

Bible Story: *Paul escapes* – **Read Acts 9:25 and 2 Corinthians 11:33.**

Lesson 84   Name:

Draw a picture of Paul's escape and then write about it. Use as many spelling words as you can.

| out | about | down | yellow | Paul | yawn | one |
| our | house | now | bowl | saw | straw | from |

Paul Escapes in a Basket

Check-up time   Lesson 85   Name:

Spelling Test	Corrections	Practice
1.		1.
2.		2.
3.		3.
4.		4.
5.		5.
6.		6.
7.		7.
8.		8.
9.		9.
10.		10.
11.		11.
12.		12.
13.		13.
14.		14.

Check-up time   Lesson 85   Name:

Test Again

More Practice

Horizons Spelling Grade 1

What do you know?

Lessons 86–90   **Name:**

Write the words your teacher reads.

Words for the Week	Corrections	Practice
1.		1.
2.		2.
3.		3.
4.		4.
5.		5.
6.		6.
7.		7.
8.		8.
9.		9.
10.		10.
11.		11.
12.		12.
13.		13.
14.		14.

Words for the Week

boy	joy	join	birthday	airport	football	thank
toy	boil	noise	butterfly	mailman	rainbow	four

1 Write two sentences using your spelling words.

2 Practice your spelling words. Don't forget your working words.

Horizons Spelling Grade 1

Lesson 86   Name: _____

oi, oy, Compound Words

1. **Write the oy and oi words.**

oy   oi

_____   _____

_____   _____

_____   _____

2. **Write the compound words.**

_____ + _____ = _____

_____ + _____ = _____

_____ + _____ = _____

_____ + _____ = _____

Spelling Words

boy

toy

joy

boil

join

noise

birthday

butterfly

airport

mailman

football

rainbow

Working Words

thank

four

Spelling Spotlight

Lesson 87

Name: _____

boy	joy	join	birthday	airport	football	thank
toy	boil	noise	butterfly	mailman	rainbow	four

1 Write the word. Draw a line to the picture.

1. you play with this _____

2. loud sound _____

3. 3 + 1 = _____

4. he brings the mail _____

5. airplanes land here _____

6. put together _____

7. happiness _____

 2 Write the spelling word for the picture.

_____

_____

_____

Horizons Spelling Grade 1

Lesson 88

Name: _____

butterfly   football   rainbow   thank

 Answer the question. Use a sentence.

What spelling word is both a game and a kind of ball?

_____

What do you say when someone helps you?

_____

What hatches from a cocoon?

_____

What do we sometimes see after a rain storm?

_____

Bible Story: *The Story of Noah* – Genesis chapters 6–9 (especially 9:13–16).
Read the story and color the picture.

Lesson 89

1 Draw a rainbow.

2 Write about a rainbow you have seen.

Lesson 90

Name: _____

Spelling Test	Corrections	Practice
1.		1.
2.		2.
3.		3.
4.		4.
5.		5.
6.		6.
7.		7.
8.		8.
9.		9.
10.		10.
11.		11.
12.		12.
13.		13.
14.		14.

Check-up time   Lesson 90   Name:

Test Again

More Practice

Horizons Spelling Grade 1

What do you know

Name: _____

Write the words your teacher reads.

Words for the Week	Corrections	Practice
1.		1.
2.		2.
3.		3.
4.		4.
5.		5.
6.		6.
7.		7.
8.		8.
9.		9.
10.		10.
11.		11.
12.		12.
13.		13.
14.		14.

Words for the Week

plant	glass	sleep	brown	green	drop	five
bless	clock	fly	free	pray	frog	six

1 Write two sentences using your spelling words.

_____

_____

_____

_____

2 Practice your spelling words. Don't forget your working words.

Lesson 91
l blends, r blends

Name: _____

1 **Circle the word and write it.**

xflyd _____

tprayxl _____

bglassz _____

ydropb _____

gfreed _____

tclockzy _____

bplantty _____

xfivet _____

dbrownm _____

zsleepbt _____

2 **Write your working words.**

_____ _____

_____ _____

_____ _____

Spelling Words

plant

bless

glass

clock

sleep

fly

brown

free

green

pray

drop

frog

Working Words

five

six

Lesson 92   Name:

| plant | glass | sleep | brown | green | drop | five |
| bless | clock | fly | free | pray | frog | six |

1 Write a spelling word that rhymes.

yes _____   seen _____

log _____   mix _____

hive _____   class _____

knock _____   my _____

day _____   town _____

can't _____   stop _____

tree _____   weep _____

2 Write two number words.

_____   _____

3 Write two color words.

_____   _____

Spelling Spotlight

Lesson 93   Name:

1. Write the words.

plant

bless

glass

clock

sleep

fly

brown

free

green

pray

drop

frog

five

six

ACROSS:
1. An insect.
2. The color of grass.
4. Pray and praise.
5. What you do at night.
8. The color of a tree trunk.

DOWN:
1. No cost.
2. Used for a drink.
3. Tells the time.
6. Something that grows.
7. It jumps and makes a funny noise.

2. Write the word.

4 + 1 = _____   talk to God _____

3 + 3 = _____   let some-   _____
thing fall

Bible Verse: I will bless the Lord at all times.

Psalm 34:1

Horizons Spelling Grade 1   153

Lesson 94

Name: _____

plant	glass	sleep	brown	green	drop	five
bless	clock	fly	free	pray	frog	six

Write a sentence. Draw a picture. Use the spelling words.

green   frog

_____

pray   bless

_____

sleep   clock

_____

glass   drop

_____

Horizons Spelling Grade 1

Check-up time Lesson 95 Name:

Spelling Test	Corrections	Practice
1.		1.
2.		2.
3.		3.
4.		4.
5.		5.
6.		6.
7.		7.
8.		8.
9.		9.
10.		10.
11.		11.
12.		12.
13.		13.
14.		14.

Check-up time   Lesson 95   Name:

Test Again	More Practice

Write the words your teacher reads.

Words for the Week	Corrections	Practice
1.		1.
2.		2.
3.		3.
4.		4.
5.		5.
6.		6.
7.		7.
8.		8.
9.		9.
10.		10.
11.		11.
12.		12.
13.		13.
14.		14.

Words for the Week

snow   slip   skip   snake   street   smell   Easter
stop   smoke   speak   stove   snail   sky   after

1 Write two sentences using your spelling words.

_____

_____

_____

_____

2 Practice your spelling words. Don't forget your working words.

Horizons Spelling Grade 1

Lesson 96 Name: _____

st, sl, sm, sn, sk, sp Words

1 Write a spelling word that rhymes. Draw a line to the picture.

rake _____

pail _____

go _____

mop _____

joke _____

greet _____

weak _____

fly _____

2 Write your working words.

_____ _____

_____ _____

Spelling Words

snow

stop

slip

smoke

skip

speak

snake

stove

street

snail

smell

sky

Working Words

Easter

after

Lesson 97

Name: _____

1. Put the words in **ABC** order.

Easter
after
slip
skip
stove
smell

1. _____   4. _____

2. _____   5. _____

3. _____   6. _____

snow   slip   skip   snake   street   smell   Easter
stop   smoke   speak   stove   snail   sky   after

2. Finish the words.

sn _____   sk _____   __ a __ e

s __ o _____   s l _____   s _____

s _____   __ o __ e __   s _____

s _____   s _____   s _____

3. Write the working word shapes.

_____ _____

_____ _____

Write a sentence using spelling words.

snail   stop   street

stove   smoke   smell

snake   slip   snow

sky   speak   skip

Easter   after

Bible Story: *The Easter Story* – Matthew 28, Mark 16, Luke 24, or John 20.

Lesson 99

Name: _____

✏️ **Draw and write.**

| Easter | rose | angels | Peter | Jesus | stone | Mary |

The First Easter

Spelling Test	Corrections	Practice
1.		1.
2.		2.
3.		3.
4.		4.
5.		5.
6.		6.
7.		7.
8.		8.
9.		9.
10.		10.
11.		11.
12.		12.
13.		13.
14.		14.

Check-up time

Lesson 100   Name:

Test Again	More Practice

Horizons Spelling Grade 1

Write the words your teacher reads.

Words for the Week	Corrections	Practice
1.		1.
2.		2.
3.		3.
4.		4.
5.		5.
6.		6.
7.		7.
8.		8.
9.		9.
10.		10.
11.		11.
12.		12.
13.		13.
14.		14.

Words for the Week

that	their	then	she	shell	ship	seven
there	them	this	she	shall	sheep	shoe	nine

1 Write two sentences using your spelling words.

2 Practice your spelling words. Don't forget your working words.

Horizons Spelling Grade 1

Lesson 101
th, sh Words

Name: _____

1. Write the **th** and **sh** words.

th	sh

2. Write the number words.

7   **9**

_____   _____

3. Write your other working words.

_____   _____

Spelling Words

that

there

their

them

then

this

she

shall

shell

sheep

ship

shoe

Working Words

seven

nine

---

that	their	then	she	shell	ship	seven
there	them	this	she	shall	sheep	ship	shoe	nine

1. Write the spelling word.

1. a big boat _____

2. an animal _____

3. found on a beach _____

4. 5 + 2 = _____

5. worn on a foot _____

6. 6 + 3 = _____

7. rhymes with **when** _____

8. rhymes with **pal** _____

2. Write three words used for people.

_____ _____ _____

3. Write three words used to point out something.

_____ _____ _____

✏️ **Circle the word and write it on the line.**

1. Please put _____ book over _____ .
           this   then   there   their

2. I like _____ white house.
       them   that

3. Joan and Bob left _____ jackets at home.
          there   their

4. We will go to church with _____ .
          them   then

5. First, we work. _____ , we rest.
          Them   Then

6. I _____ go home when _____ comes home.
      shell   shall   ship   she

 Bible Story: *The Good Shepherd* – Luke 15:4–6 and John 10:11–18.
             Read the story and color the picture.

Lesson 104 Name: _____

Write a story and draw a picture about Jesus, the Good Shepherd.

Jesus   shepherd   good   lost   sheep   happy

The Good Shepherd

Spelling Test	Corrections	Practice
1.		1.
2.		2.
3.		3.
4.		4.
5.		5.
6.		6.
7.		7.
8.		8.
9.		9.
10.		10.
11.		11.
12.		12.
13.		13.
14.		14.

Test Again

More Practice

What do you know

Name: --

Write the words your teacher reads.

Words for the Week	Corrections	Practice
1.		1.
2.		2.
3.		3.
4.		4.
5.		5.
6.		6.
7.		7.
8.		8.
9.		9.
10.		10.
11.		11.
12.		12.
13.		13.
14.		14.

Words for the Week

church   chin   lunch   Christ   school   stick   because
child   much   children   echo   pack   lock   been

1 Write two sentences using your spelling words.

2 Practice your spelling words. Don't forget your working words.

What do you know

Lesson 106
ch- and -ck Words

Name: _____

Match the spelling words with their shapes.

 church

 child

 children

chin

 lunch

much

 Christ

echo

 school

lock

 pack

stick

Spelling Words
church
child
chin
much
lunch
children
Christ
echo
school
pack
stick
lock

Working Words
because
been

Horizons Spelling Grade 1

175

🔍 **What sounds do you hear?**

church   chin   lunch   Christ   school   stick   because
child   much   children   echo   pack   lock   been

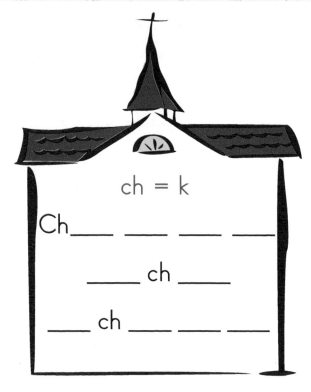

ch = k

Ch___ ___ ___ ___

___ ch ___

___ ch ___ ___

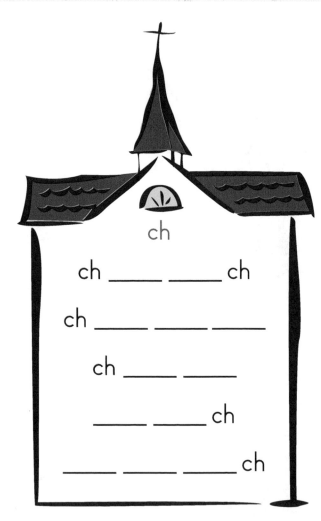

ch

ch ___ ___ ch

ch ___ ___ ___

ch ___ ___

___ ___ ch

___ ___ ___ ch

ck = k

___ ___ ___ ck

___ ___ ck

___ ___ ck

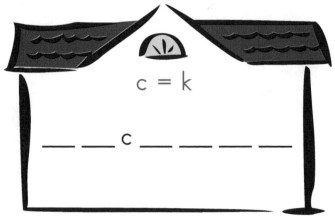

c = k

___ ___ c ___ ___ ___

Spelling Spotlight

Lesson 108   Name:

Write a sentence with the spelling words.

school   lunch   pack

church   Christ   children

child   echo

stick   lock

much   chin

Bible Verse: Let the little children come to me.

Luke 18:16

✏ **Color the picture. Write a sentence that tells how Christ loves little children.**

Check-up time

Lesson 110

Name: _____

Spelling Test	Corrections	Practice
1.		1.
2.		2.
3.		3.
4.		4.
5.		5.
6.		6.
7.		7.
8.		8.
9.		9.
10.		10.
11.		11.
12.		12.
13.		13.
14.		14.

Test Again

More Practice

What do you know

Name: _____

Write the words your teacher reads.

Words for the Week	Corrections	Practice
1.		1.
2.		2.
3.		3.
4.		4.
5.		5.
6.		6.
7.		7.
8.		8.
9.		9.
10.		10.
11.		11.
12.		12.
13.		13.
14.		14.

Words for the Week

who	when	which	match	itch	patch	under
what	where	whale	pitch	watch	latch	until

1 Write two sentences using your spelling words.

---

2 Practice your spelling words. Don't forget your working words.

Horizons Spelling Grade 1

Lesson 111

wh-, -tch Words

Name: _____

1. Write the three ___ *atch* words that rhyme.

_____

_____

_____

2. Write the spelling words that ask a question.

_____ ?   _____ ?

_____ ?   _____ ?

_____ ?

3. Write the spelling word for the picture.

_____   _____

4. Write your working words.

_____   _____

Spelling Words

who
what
when
where
which
whale
match
pitch
itch
watch
patch
latch

Working Words

under
until

Spelling Spotlight

Lesson 112   Name: _____

Circle the spelling words. Write them on the lines.

```
p  a  t  c  h  x  d  w  r
i  m  a  t  c  h  v  h  z
t  w  h  e  r  e  w  a  n
c  w  l  i  v  p  h  l  o
h  h  a  t  w  o  i  e  x
w  a  t  c  h  x  c  u  m
h  t  c  h  e  m  h  n  p
o  z  h  w  n  i  t  d  s
r  w  b  l  x  v  m  e  t
u  n  t  i  l  p  d  r  o
```

✏ **Make a question.**

Who	What	Where	When	Which

1. _____ time is it?

2. _____ book will you read?

3. _____ will it be time to go?

4. _____ is the box of toys?

5. _____ is coming to visit us?

Bible Verse: Who do the crowds say I am? Who do you say I am?
                                    Luke 9:18–20
Write the verse and answer the question: Who do you say that Jesus is?

_____

_____

_____

_____

_____

_____

_____

_____

Lesson 114

Name: _____

 Finish the rhymes.

| latch | itch | until | pitch | whale |

When he threw the _____,

he had an _____.

When you close the hatch,

don't forget the _____.

I had a pail

too small for a _____.

Wait _____

we climb the hill.

Lesson 115   Name: _____

Spelling Test	Corrections	Practice
1.		1.
2.		2.
3.		3.
4.		4.
5.		5.
6.		6.
7.		7.
8.		8.
9.		9.
10.		10.
11.		11.
12.		12.
13.		13.
14.		14.

Check-up time   Lesson 115   Name:

Test Again

More Practice

Horizons Spelling Grade 1

What do you remember

Name: ------------------------------------

Write the words your teacher reads.

1. _____

2. _____

3. _____

4. _____

5. _____

6. _____

7. _____

8. _____

9. _____

10. _____

11. _____

12. _____

13. _____

14. _____

15. _____

16. _____

17. _____

18. _____

19. _____

20. _____

21. _____

22. _____

23. _____

24. _____

25. _____

26. _____

27. _____

28. _____

Review Words

our	thank	sleep	after	there	because	under
about	for	pray	stop	their	church	when
from	joy	bless	sky	them	Christ	where
house	rainbow	green	street	that	children	what

Practice your review words.

Spelling Spotlight

Lesson 116
Review

Name: _____

our	thank	sleep	after	there	because	under
about	for	pray	stop	their	church	when
from	joy	bless	sky	them	Christ	where
house	rainbow	green	street	that	children	what

1 Put the words in **ABC** order.

Christ
about
pray
sky
children
sleep
rainbow
them

1. _____

2. _____

3. _____

4. _____

5. _____

6. _____

7. _____

8. _____

2 Write the word that rhymes.

flower _____

fat _____

mouse _____

ten _____

boy _____

dress _____

 Unscramble the picture word and write it on the line.

osuhe

nereg

tpos

retest

hcruhc

nairwob

----

2 **Circle the correct word.**

1. We came home (**for** **from**) the store.

2. Did you see (**that** **there**) dog hiding (**what** **under**) the table?

3. We (**this** **thank**) God (**pray** **because**) He loves us.

4. (**What** **Where**) did you go last night?

5. We (**sleep** **pray**) in (**church** **rainbow**).

6. Will (**there** **their**) mother be (**their** **there**)?

Spelling
Spotlight

Lesson 118   Name: _____

1 Write a question with the words.

What _____ ?

When _____ ?

Where _____ ?

2 Recall the Bible story in each picture and write a sentence about it.

_____
_____
_____
_____
_____

_____
_____
_____
_____
_____

Lesson 119   Name: _____

1 Write a story using the spelling words in the box.

_____

- -

_____

- -

_____

- -

_____

- -

_____

2 Draw a picture about your story.

Horizons Spelling Grade 1

Check-up time

Lesson 120   Name: _____

Write the words your teacher reads.

1.	13.	25.
2.	14.	26.
3.	15.	27.
4.	16.	28.
5.	17.	
6.	18.	
7.	19.	
8.	20.	
9.	21.	
10.	22.	
11.	23.	
12.	24.	

Check-up time

Lesson 120

Name: _____

Test Again	More Practice

Name: --

Write the words your teacher reads.

Words for the Week	Corrections	Practice
1.		1.
2.		2.
3.		3.
4.		4.
5.		5.
6.		6.
7.		7.
8.		8.
9.		9.
10.		10.
11.		11.
12.		12.
13.		13.
14.		14.

1 Write two sentences using your spelling words.

_____

- -

_____

- -

_____

2 Practice your spelling words. Don't forget your working words.

Spelling Spotlight

Lesson 121   Name: _____

Synonyms

1. Circle the spelling words. Write the words.

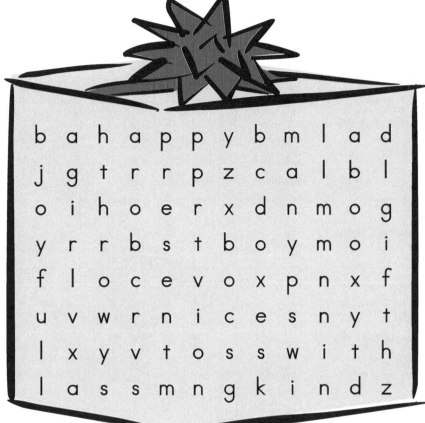

```
b a h a p p y b m l a d
j g t r r p z c a l b l
o i h o e r x d n m o g
y r r b s t b o y m o i
f l o c e v o x p n x f
u v w r n i c e s n y t
l x y v t o s s w i t h
l a s s m n g k i n d z
```

Spelling Words

happy
joyful
kind
nice
gift
present
girl
lass
boy
lad
toss
throw

Working Words

many
with

happy	kind	gift	girl	boy	toss	many
joyful	nice	present	lass	lad	throw	with

1 Write four spelling words for people.

2 Write two words for how you can feel.

3 Write two words for things you can do.

4 Write two words for the way you can be toward others.

5 Write two words for something you can give to someone.

6 Write a word for more than 5 or 6.

7 Fill in the spelling word.

Will you play _____ me?

Horizons Spelling Grade 1

Spelling Spotlight

Lesson 123   Name: _____

✏ **Use the words in a sentence. Draw a picture.**

| happy   present   girl |

_____
_____
_____
_____

| boy   nice   toss |

_____
_____
_____
_____

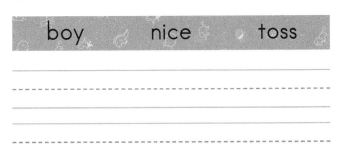

| lass   joyful   kind |

_____
_____
_____
_____

 Bible Verse: Love is patient. Love is kind.   1 Cor. 13:4
Write the verse. Write something kind you can do.

_____
_____
_____

Lesson 124 Name:

1 **Finish the sentences.**

I am happy when

The little lad

The surprise gift was

The children were joyful because

The boy will throw

Horizons Spelling Grade 1

Check-up time   Lesson 125   Name: _____

Spelling Test	Corrections	Practice
1.		1.
2.		2.
3.		3.
4.		4.
5.		5.
6.		6.
7.		7.
8.		8.
9.		9.
10.		10.
11.		11.
12.		12.
13.		13.
14.		14.

Check-up time

Lesson 125　Name: _____

Test Again	More Practice

Horizons Spelling Grade 1

Name: --

Write the words your teacher reads.

Words for the Week	Corrections	Practice
1.		1.
2.		2.
3.		3.
4.		4.
5.		5.
6.		6.
7.		7.
8.		8.
9.		9.
10.		10.
11.		11.
12.		12.
13.		13.
14.		14.

Words for the Week

white	hot	more	long	thick	big	never
black	cold	less	short	thin	little	always

1 **Write two sentences using your spelling words.**

_____

_____

_____

_____

_____

_____

2 **Practice your spelling words. Don't forget your working words.**

Horizons Spelling Grade 1

✎ **Unscramble and write the words.**

gib	ttille
_____	_____
lgno	orsht
_____	_____
vener	wayals
_____	_____
kcith	niht
_____	_____
rome	ssel
_____	_____
toh	ldoc
_____	_____
hweit	clakb
_____	_____

Spelling Words

white
black
hot
cold
more
less
long
short
thick
thin
big
little

Working Words

never
always

Spelling Spotlight

Lesson 127   Name:

hot	little	cold	thin
white	big	thick	long

✏ Finish the sentences.

Snow is _____ .

The sun is _____ .

Ice is _____ .

A whale is _____ .

A bug is _____ .

The wall is _____ .

The boy is _____ .

The road is _____ .

CITY
1 MILE

Spelling Spotlight

Lesson 128   Name: _____

1 Circle the word and write it in the sentence.

1. more
   less

   John has _____ blocks than Judy.

2. more
   less

   Betty has _____ pencils than Bill.

3. always
   never

   Jesus will _____ love us.

4. always
   never

   We should _____ do anything to hurt Jesus.

Bible Story: *David and Goliath* – 1 Samuel 17 (especially v. 37–51).
Color the picture.

Lesson 129 Name: ----------------------------------

| hot cold | big little | thick thin | more less | black white | long short | never always |

1 Pick two sets of spelling words and write a story.

2 Draw a picture of your story.

Check-up time

Lesson 130

Name: _____

Spelling Test	Corrections	Practice
1.		1.
2.		2.
3.		3.
4.		4.
5.		5.
6.		6.
7.		7.
8.		8.
9.		9.
10.		10.
11.		11.
12.		12.
13.		13.
14.		14.

Lesson 130

Name: _____

Test Again	More Practice

What do you know ?

Name: ---

Write the words your teacher reads.

Words for the Week	Corrections	Practice
1.		1.
2.		2.
3.		3.
4.		4.
5.		5.
6.		6.
7.		7.
8.		8.
9.		9.
10.		10.
11.		11.
12.		12.
13.		13.
14.		14.

Words for the Week

to	weak	meet	peek	road	ate	look
two	week	meat	peak	rode	eight	something

1 Write two sentences using your spelling words.

_____

_____

_____

_____

2 Practice your spelling words. Don't forget your working words.

Horizons Spelling Grade 1

 Match the words and pictures.

peek

peak

meet

meat

road

rode

ate

eight

week

weak

SUNDAY
MONDAY
TUESDAY
WEDNESDAY
THURSDAY
FRIDAY
SATURDAY

8

 Write your working words.

_____   _____

_____   _____

_____   _____

Spelling Words

to
two
weak
week
meet
meat
peek
peak
road
rode
ate
eight

Working Words

look
something

Spelling Spotlight

Lesson 132 Name: _____

to	weak	meet	peek	road	ate	look
two	week	meat	peak	rode	eight	something

1 Write the four spelling words that rhyme.

_____ _____

_____ _____

2 Finish the sentences.

1. I took _____ books _____ school.

2. This _____ I felt very _____ .

3. We will _____ to eat some _____ .

4. Take a _____ at the mountain _____ .

5. Jim _____ his horse down the _____ .

6. We _____ dinner at _____ .

7. Here is _____ to _____ at.

Spelling Spotlight

Lesson 133   Name: _____

 Write the spelling words in the puzzle.

to
two
weak
week
meet
meat
peek
peak
road
rode
ate
eight

ACROSS:
1. sickly
2. 8
4. done riding
5. look into
6. path or street
8. chicken or beef
9. move toward

DOWN:
1. seven days
3. 2
5. mountain top
7. done eating
8. come together

2 Unscramble the sentences and write them. Don't forget the period!

at   park   in   me   Meet   the   eight

_____

peak   We   climb   will   the

_____

Lesson 134 Name:

Bible Story: *The Good Samaritan* – **Luke 10:30–37.**
Draw a picture and write a story telling how you can be a Good Samaritan.

I am a Good Samaritan when I

Horizons Spelling Grade 1

Check-up time   Lesson 135   Name: _____

Spelling Test	Corrections	Practice
1.		1.
2.		2.
3.		3.
4.		4.
5.		5.
6.		6.
7.		7.
8.		8.
9.		9.
10.		10.
11.		11.
12.		12.
13.		13.
14.		14.

Check-up time Lesson 135 Name:

Test Again

More Practice

What do you know?

Name: --

Write the words your teacher reads.

Words for the Week	Corrections	Practice
1.		1.
2.		2.
3.		3.
4.		4.
5.		5.
6.		6.
7.		7.
8.		8.
9.		9.
10.		10.
11.		11.
12.		12.
13.		13.
14.		14.

Words for the Week

car   farm   hard   or   story   store   knew

part   park   arm   for   forget   door   pretty

1 Write two sentences using your spelling words.

_____

_____

_____

_____

2 Practice your spelling words. Don't forget your working words.

Spelling Spotlight

Lesson 136
ar, or Words

Name: _____

Spelling Words

car
part
farm
park
hard
arm
or
for
story
forget
store
door

Working Words

knew
pretty

1 Write the *ar* words for the pictures.

_ _ _ _ _ _ _ _ _ _ _ _ _ _ _ _

_ _ _ _ _ _ _ _ _ _ _ _ _ _ _ _

_ _ _ _ _ _ _ _ _ _ _ _ _ _ _ _

2 Match the *or* words with their shapes.

or
for
story
forget
store
door

3 Write your working words.

_ _

_ _

Horizons Spelling Grade 1   223

car	farm	hard	or	story	store	knew
part	park	arm	for	forget	door	pretty

 Write a sentence using the words.

car   park

story   pretty   forget

for   store   part

door   arm

knew   or

farm   hard

| car | farm | hard | or | story | store | knew |
| part | park | arm | for | forget | door | pretty |

What does it mean? _____

1. You ride in a _____ .

2. Some animals live on a _____ .

3. Please close the _____ .

4. *Cinderella* is a _____ .

5. You buy things in a _____ .

6. A rock is very _____ .

7. Your hand is at the end of your _____ .

8. A form of the verb *know*. _____

9. Something nice to look at is _____ .

10. If you can't remember, you _____ .

11. Sounds just like 4. _____

12. Sounds just like *oar*. _____

13. A place to walk and play is a _____ .

14. A piece of something is called a _____ .

Lesson 139   Name: ------------------------------------

Bible Story: *Jesus Uses a Story to Teach* – Matthew 25:1–13.

A parable is a story that teaches us a lesson. Jesus told many parables to teach us how to live. You have learned many parables this year. Pick one from the box or another favorite and tell about it. Draw a picture.

The Good Shepherd   The Lost Sheep
The Good Samaritan   The Wise and Foolish Virgins

Horizons Spelling Grade 1

Spelling Test	Corrections	Practice
1.		1.
2.		2.
3.		3.
4.		4.
5.		5.
6.		6.
7.		7.
8.		8.
9.		9.
10.		10.
11.		11.
12.		12.
13.		13.
14.		14.

Test Again

More Practice

What do you know

Name: --

Write the words your teacher reads.

Words for the Week	Corrections	Practice
1.		1.
2.		2.
3.		3.
4.		4.
5.		5.
6.		6.
7.		7.
8.		8.
9.		9.
10.		10.
11.		11.
12.		12.
13.		13.
14.		14.

Words for the Week

first　　shirt　　third　　every　　burn　　nurse　　behind
skirt　　bird　　her　　serve　　purple　　turn　　over

1 Write two sentences using your spelling words.

2 Practice your spelling words. Don't forget your working words.

Spelling Spotlight

Lesson 141
ir, er, ur Words

Name: _____

1 Trace the word and match the picture.

ir words

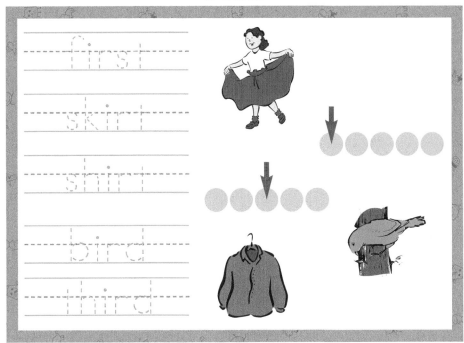

first

skirt

shirt

bird

third

ur words

burn

purple

nurse

turn

2 Write your working words.

_____   _____

_____   _____

_____   _____

Spelling Words

first

skirt

shirt

bird

third

her

every

serve

burn

purple

nurse

turn

Working Words

behind

over

Lesson 142 Name: _____

first	shirt	third	every	burn	nurse	behind
skirt	bird	her	serve	purple	turn	over

  Write the *er* words.

_____   _____

_____   _____

_____   _____

_____   _____

2 **Unscramble the words and write them.**

rdib	htrid	trish

_____   _____   _____

ursne	urnb	utrn

_____   _____   _____

reh	verey	vrese

_____   _____   _____

ristf	pleurp	krist

_____   _____   _____

vero	hebnid

_____   _____

Horizons Spelling Grade 1

Guess which word? Write the spelling word.

purple	first	nurse	turn	serve
burn	behind	third	over	bird

1. I'm number 1.

2. I like to chirp.

3. I take care of sick people.

4. Ouch! That's hot!

5. Two come before me.

6. I'm the color of grape gum.

7. I'm not in front.

8. I move around the corner.

9. I'm on top of things.

10. When I do this, I help others.

Bible Story: *Jesus came to serve others* – **John 13:1–17. Jesus washes the feet of his disciples.**

How do you serve others?

The nurse serves us by _____
_____
_____
_____
_____

We should serve others by _____
_____
_____
_____
_____

Check-up time

Lesson 145   Name: _____

Spelling Test	Corrections	Practice
1.		1.
2.		2.
3.		3.
4.		4.
5.		5.
6.		6.
7.		7.
8.		8.
9.		9.
10.		10.
11.		11.
12.		12.
13.		13.
14.		14.

Test Again	More Practice

What do you know

Lessons 146–150   Name: _____

Write the words your teacher reads.

Words for the Week	Corrections	Practice
1.		1.
2.		2.
3.		3.
4.		4.
5.		5.
6.		6.
7.		7.
8.		8.
9.		9.
10.		10.
11.		11.
12.		12.
13.		13.
14.		14.

Words for the Week

quick   quit   laugh   photo   tough   would   does

quack   queen   phone   rough   could   should   right

1   **Write two sentences using your spelling words.**

2   **Practice your spelling words. Don't forget your working words.**

1 Write the words.

qu	ph = f

gh = f	ould

igh = i	A word that rhymes with *was.*

2 Write your working words.

Spelling Words

quick
quack
quit
queen
laugh
phone
photo
rough
tough
could
would
should

Working Words

does
right

✎ **Write the spelling words in the puzzle.**

quick

quack

quit

queen

laugh

phone

photo

rough

tough

could

would

should

does

right

ACROSS:

2. I'm so tired, I'll have to _____ now.

4. If I _____ come, I would be happy.

6. The duck said, "_____."

8. The meat was too _____ to chew.

9. Al made a _____ turn.

DOWN:

1. The running boy was very _____ .

3. Jill was crowned _____ for the parade.

5. Sally looked so funny that she made me _____ .

7. The dirt road was very _____ .

| quick | quit | laugh | photo | tough | would | does |
| quack | queen | phone | rough | could | should | right |

✎ **Write a sentence for the picture. Use a spelling word.**

 Bible Story: *Queen Esther saves her people* – **Esther chapters 4–7.**

Lesson 149   Name: _____

quick   quit   laugh   photo   tough   would   does
quack   queen   phone   rough   could   should   right

Use your spelling words to write a story about a queen who would not laugh and a king who tried many things to make her laugh. Draw a picture of your story.

Horizons Spelling Grade 1

Spelling Test	Corrections	Practice
1.		1.
2.		2.
3.		3.
4.		4.
5.		5.
6.		6.
7.		7.
8.		8.
9.		9.
10.		10.
11.		11.
12.		12.
13.		13.
14.		14.

Check-up time Lesson 150 Name: _____

Test Again	More Practice

What do you know

Name: _____

Write the words your teacher reads.

Words for the Week	Corrections	Practice
1.		1.
2.		2.
3.		3.
4.		4.
5.		5.
6.		6.
7.		7.
8.		8.
9.		9.
10.		10.
11.		11.
12.		12.
13.		13.
14.		14.

Words for the Week

ball   walk   all   hugging   hopping   hoping   haven't
small   talk   hugged   hopped   begging   smiling   went

1 Write two sentences using your spelling words.

2 Practice your spelling words. Don't forget your working words.

Horizons Spelling Grade 1

1. Word forms. Write the spelling words.

hug	hop

beg	hope

smile

2. Write the contraction. _____

3. Write the words with the *al* sound.

4. Write your working words.

Spelling Words

ball
small
walk
talk
all
hugged
hugging
hopped
hopping
begging
hoping
smiling

Working Words

haven't
went

1 How words are changed. **Look at the words and finish the sentences.**

hug	hugged	hugging
hop	hopped	hopping
hope	hoped	hoping
smile	smiled	smiling

1. To make the word *hugging*, you must take the word _____ _____, double the letter _____ , and add _____ .

2. To make the word *hopped*, you must take the word _____ _____, double the letter_____ , and add_____ .

3. To make the word *smiling*, you must take the word _____ _____, drop the letter_____ , and add_____ .

4. To make the word *hoping*, you must take the word _____ _____, drop the letter_____ , and add_____ .

ball	walk	all	hugging	hopping	hoping	haven't
small	talk	hugged	hopped	begging	smiling	went

2 Write the spelling words that rhyme.

tall _____ _____ _____

chalk _____ _____

sent _____

Horizons Spelling Grade 1

Lesson 153   Name: _____

Circle the correct word and write it in the sentence.

1. Julie was _____ down the path.
   hoping   hopping

2. Sam was _____ at the little child.
   smiling   smileing

3. The poor man was _____ for some food.
   beging   begging

4. Molly was _____ for a new bike.
   hoping   hoped

5. Beth _____ her new teddy bear.
   hugging   hugged

6. The _____ _____ bounced down the street.
   all   ball   small

7. Sally will _____ to _____ of the children.
   talk   walk   ball   all

8. Jesus could _____ on the water.
   talk   walk

9. Johnny kept_____ his mother when she came home.
   hugged   hugging

Bible Story: *Jesus cures the blind beggar – Luke 18:35-43.*

Lesson 154 Name: _____

Study the picture. Write a story about what you might see as you walk through the park. Finish the picture with things in your story.

A Walk in the Park

Spelling Test

1.
2.
3.
4.
5.
6.
7.
8.
9.
10.
11.
12.
13.
14.

Corrections

Practice

1.
2.
3.
4.
5.
6.
7.
8.
9.
10.
11.
12.
13.
14.

Check-up time

Lesson 155

Name: _____

Test Again	More Practice

Horizons Spelling Grade 1

 **What do you remember** Lessons 117–155   **Name:** _____

Write the words your teacher reads.

1. _____   13. _____   25. _____

2. _____   14. _____   26. _____

3. _____   15. _____   27. _____

4. _____   16. _____   28. _____

5. _____   17. _____   _____

6. _____   18. _____   _____

7. _____   19. _____   _____

8. _____   20. _____   _____

9. _____   21. _____   _____

10. _____   22. _____   _____

11. _____   23. _____   _____

12. _____   24. _____   _____

Review Words

happy	always	something	pretty	over	right	went
many	never	to	knew	behind	quick	haven't
with	little	two	for	every	would	all
kind	more	eight	story	first	should	smiling

Practice your review words.

Spelling Spotlight

Lesson 156
Review

Name: _____

happy	always	something	pretty	over	right	went
many	never	to	knew	behind	quick	haven't
with	little	two	for	every	would	all
kind	more	eight	story	first	should	smiling

1 **Write the word.**

8 _____

fast _____

2 _____

tiny _____

nice _____

lovely _____

2 **Write the spelling word that is opposite.**

under _____

none _____

sad _____

frowning _____

nothing _____

in front _____

have _____

last _____

left _____

never _____

Lesson 157 Name: _____

 Put the words in ABC order.

| behind |
| went |
| to |
| right |
| all |
| every |
| with |
| two |
| quick |
| should |

1. _____   6. _____

2. _____   7. _____

3. _____   8. _____

4. _____   9. _____

5. _____   10. _____

2 **Draw a line to match the word with its shape.**

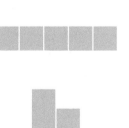

many

with

never

more

to

knew

for

story

every

would

should

went

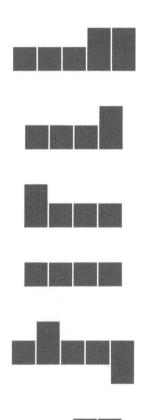

Horizons Spelling Grade 1

Lesson 158   Name:

✏ **Unscramble the sentences and write them. Don't forget the period!**

the	story	Kate	knew

made	The	Bill	present	happy

kind	would	John	be	always

than	Al	food	did	more	had	I

had	doll	little	Mary	a	pretty

✝ **Write a sentence about your favorite Bible story or Bible verse.**

happy	always	something	pretty	over	right	went
many	never	to	knew	behind	quick	haven't
with	little	two	for	every	would	all
kind	more	eight	story	first	should	smiling

Draw a picture of yourself and write a story about your year in first grade. Use as many spelling words as you can.

Write the words your teacher reads.

1. _____   13. _____   25. _____

2. _____   14. _____   26. _____

3. _____   15. _____   27. _____

4. _____   16. _____   28. _____

5. _____   17. _____   _____

6. _____   18. _____   _____

7. _____   19. _____   _____

8. _____   20. _____   _____

9. _____   21. _____   _____

10. _____   22. _____   _____

11. _____   23. _____   _____

12. _____   24. _____   _____

Check-up time

Lesson 160   Name:

Test Again	More Practice

Horizons Spelling Grade 1